There's Just Something About a Boy

There's Just Something About a Boy

ISBN: 978-1-60920-036-7
Printed in the United States of America
©2011 by Jenny Lee Sulpizio
All rights reserved

Illustrations by Peg Lozier

Layout and cover design by Ajoyin Publishing, Inc.

Library of Congress Cataloging-in-Publication Data

API
Ajoyin Publishing, Inc.
P.O. 342
Three Rivers, MI 49093
www.ajoyin.com

Please direct your inquiries to admin@ajoyin.com

There's Just Something About a Boy

Jenny Lee Sulpizio   Illustrated by Peg Lozier

Dedication

For my handsome, strong-willed, vivacious blessings–Ketch and Rook

You'll spread your wings and away you'll soar,
You'll have bumps, bruises, challenges, and more.
But I'll sit back quietly and watch your lives start,
Armed with your faith and His words in your heart.

May you continue to live in His Word and become the men God intended
you to be. I love you, boys!

Jeremiah 29:11
J.L.S

To my fabulous niece and nephews; Tim, John, Carrie and Robert,
who always welcome me at the kid's table.

P.L.

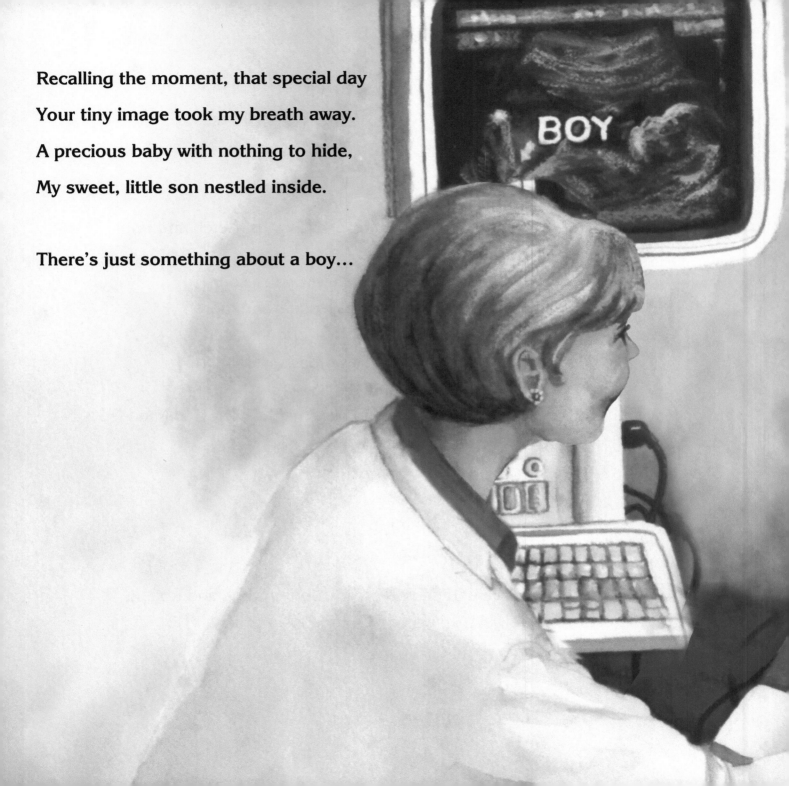

Recalling the moment, that special day
Your tiny image took my breath away.
A precious baby with nothing to hide,
My sweet, little son nestled inside.

There's just something about a boy…

I prepared your nursery
since around month five,
Waiting for the day
you'd finally arrive.
Stuffed animals, blankies,
your daddy's first glove–
They sat in your room,
awaiting your love.

There's just something
about a boy...

Then the day came when our eyes first met;

Overcome with emotion, I wept and I wept.

A gift I was given when God sent you to me,

A beautiful boy, my sweet baby.

There's just something about a boy...

And now as I hold you close to me,

Can't help but think of all you might be.

Hopes and dreams, a mother's wishes and more,

Can't wait to see what lies in store.

There's just something about a boy…

You'll grow up fast and before I can blink

You'll be running, jumping, and raising a stink.

My baby no longer, in his place will land

A boy with behavior I can't understand.

There's just something about a boy...

Trucks and trains and cars that go vroom,

Robots and rockets–they'll live in your room

From morning 'till bedtime, you'll be on the "go,"

But I'll stay by your side as you play with them so.

There's just something about a boy...

Before I know it, kindergarten will come,

A backpack, a lunch box, you'll even sneak gum.

I'll watch as your teacher leads you inside,

As you wave goodbye with a smile so wide.

There's just something about a boy...

And in an instant, you'll grow even more

You'll love football, baseball, and raise your team's score.

I'll watch in the stands as you play with pure heart,

Your biggest cheerleader, a fan from the start.

There's just something about a boy...

In Daddy's old truck, me in the passenger seat;

Teaching you to drive will be no small feat.

Speeding too fast, taking turns too quick,

You'll be a racecar driver armed with a stick.

There's just something about a boy...

The next thing you know, I'll be snapping away

Pictures of you on graduation day.

You'll start your journey with a future so bright

I'll hold back tears and let you take flight.

There's just something about a boy…

But from this mother's hopes and dreams

There's only one wish I have it seems:

Stay here in my arms as I rock you to sleep

Save the growing for later, my baby I'll keep…

And while I'm here, God, watch over this boy,

Remind him he's special, a source of pure joy,

A gift I was given when You sent him to me,

My sweet little boy he will always be.

There's just something about a boy.

CPSIA information can be obtained
at www.ICGtesting.com
Printed in the USA
LVHW070749201021
700921LV00001B/2

9 781609 200367